CREDIT SCORE

By Jordan Riches

Table of Contents

Introduction 1
Learn the Lingo 5
15 Things to Know About Credit 7
What is a Good Credit Score? 14
   Credit Score Ranges 15
      FICO Ratings 15
      VantageScore Ratings 17
   Understanding Credit Scores 19
   Business Credit Scores 20
The Benefits of a Good Credit Score 23
   Lower Interest Rates 23
   Negotiating Possibilities 24
   Improved Chance of Credit Approval 25
   Great Credit Card Offers 25
   Better Insurance Rates 26
   Better Rental Agreements 27
   Fewer Security Deposits 28
   Self-Confidence 29
   Benefits of Good Business Credit 29
Factors Affecting Your Credit Score 33
   FICO Factors 33
      Payment History 33
      Amounts Owed 35
      Credit Length History 36

>   Recent Credit 38
>   Credit Variety 39
>   VantageScore Factors 40
>   Payment History 40
>   Type and Age of Credit..40
>   Percentage of Credit Limit Used 41
>   Total balances and debt 41
>   Recent Credit Actions and Inquiries 42
>   Available Credit 43
>   Business Credit Score Calculations 43
> Checking Your Credit Record and Score 46
>   Reasons to Check Your Credit Report...................49
>   Rejected Credit Application 49
>   Identity Fraud and Theft......................................50
>   Preparing for a Loan Application.......................51
>   Surety and Cosigning Concerns 51
>   Free Credit Checks..53
>   Checking Business Credit Scores 54
> Building Credit When You Don't Have a Credit Record..57
>   Getting Credit for the First Time 59
>   Responsible Credit Use...62
> Maximizing Your Credit Score 67
>   Improving Your Payment History Weighting.......67
>   Improving Your Amounts Owed Weighting 68

- Improving Your Credit History Length Weighting 69
- Improving Your Credit Mix Weighting 69
- Improving Your New Credit and Inquiries Weighting 70
- Increase Your Credit Score Quickly 71

How to Avoid Things that Lower Your Credit Score 73

Credit Score Myths 78
- Myths about Demographics and Personal Characteristics 80
- Myths about New Credit 81
- Myths about Credit Score Factors 83
- Myths about Bad Credit 84
- Other Myths 86

Credit Counseling and Financial Advising 89
- Signs you may need Credit Counselling 89
- Services offered by Credit Counsellors 91
- Advantages of Credit Counselling 92
- Disadvantages of Credit Counselling 93
- Finding a Reputable Credit Counsellor 94

Final Thoughts 100

Introduction

Peter is a 30-year old mechanic who rents an apartment with a credit score of 436. He has been having fun a lot lately and enjoys going out with his mates. This situation has caused him to incur more expenses than what his budget allows. Peter's salary is not enough to cover all his expenses and he has started to pay his bills when they are past due. During the last two months, Peter has used his savings and credit card to purchase groceries, pay for utilities, and cover his rent. But this month is different, and Peter has some tough decisions to make. He only has a few hundred dollars left and knows it is not enough to cover his monthly expenses – something is not getting paid this month. Will he skip his rent payment? Will he go without utilities? Will he finally break his spending habits? How can he cover all his costs when there just isn't any money left? And how will he pay back all his debts?

Mary and Joe recently got married and want to buy the house of their dreams. They know that their income must be pooled to afford the home they want, and thus they will co-sign a mortgage agreement. Both have stable jobs and they work according to a strict budget. To ensure they get home loan approval, Mary suggests that they request their credit records from Experian. Upon receiving their credit records, Joe finds that he has a credit score of 790, and Mary has a credit score of 565. Mary carefully critiques her credit record and identifies areas to improve her credit score. One year later, Joe's credit score is 820, and Mary has increased her credit score to 650. The couple has also managed to save $15,000 for a down payment on a house. The higher credit scores help them to secure a mortgage with a low interest rate and they move into their brand new home.

How do you spend your money? Are you a Peter who is quickly tumbling over the edge? Or are you representative of Mary and Joe, who take their credit seriously? You may be somewhere in the middle of these two scenarios. Regardless, this book is for you – the person who needs to start getting serious about credit.

Money – it makes the world go round… or so they say. Millions of people across the world are indebted, which means credit actually makes the world go round. Countries across the world are in debt, a lot of debt, and Americans are no different. Both governments and private people owe money to others.

Approximately 90% of people own a credit card and use it more often than is good for them. Most families are fueled by debt and have an average credit card balance of $8,500. Many people owe even more money, especially if they have two or more credit cards. Altogether, American credit card spending is in excess of $1 trillion per year. By the end of the year,

Americans will still owe at least $500 billion in credit card debts. This spending means that disposable income is now being used to pay back debts rather than saving money.

Most people already have many bills to pay each month. Adding credit card expenses onto these bills makes it even more difficult to get the most out of your salary every month. Some people also have home loans or need to pay for vehicle financing. If your credit and spending aren't managed by a strict budget, then you may find yourself in trouble quite quickly. In many cases, individuals start to have issues paying their bills and eventually use credit cards for everyday expenses. In other circumstances, people choose to skip paying some of the bills or pay their accounts later than the due date. This situation can spiral out of control at a rate much faster than you can pay back your debts.

Financial institutions know that people cannot manage their spending, but banks do not like to lose money. For this reason, financial institutions and banks started to use credit scores and credit records. The credit scoring systems make it easier for lenders to know how people use their available credit, and if you are making repayments on amounts owed to companies.

Your credit score is a number that shows how well you handle your debts. The higher is your score, the better you are at managing your debts. The credit score goes hand-in-hand with a credit report (or record). Your credit record will show how much money you owe to institutions, a list of your creditors and your payment history. It will also indicate any public filings against your name. All of this information is combined to obtain a credit score for you as an individual. A good credit score is important if you want to secure vehicle financing or a mortgage at a later point in time.

Credit card swiping is out of control and loans compound the problem. Forecasters estimate that at least one family out of every hundred families will file for bankruptcy each year. Don't become one of the statistics! Now is the time to change and become a responsible credit user. You have already picked up this book, and we will guide you through the process of credit success!

This book does not contain all the answers for how to manage your finances, or how to get rid of credit. But, the aim of this book is to provide you with information on good credit management, and how to improve your credit score. The strategies outlined in the text may help you to think more about how you are using your credit card, and give you a guideline for using credit in the future.

Each chapter will explain an aspect of credit scoring. The book starts with some definitions used throughout the book; you can refer back to the terminology at any time if you are uncertain about a word. The following chapters will discuss good credit scores and the benefit of having a high credit score.

Further chapters discuss the calculation of credit scores and the importance of checking your credit record. We will also look at obtaining credit for the first time, how to maximize your score, and things to avoid that lower your credit score. The final chapters discuss myths about credit scores and explain credit counseling as a credit control strategy.

Learn the Lingo

Terminology can be quite a daunting thing, especially when you are trying to wrap your head around new concepts. To make it easier for you, we have compiled a list of the terms (words) frequently used in this book. This list is great to reference back to when you are uncertain about a specific concept or need clarification.

Bankruptcy: a process administered by the courts when a person can no longer pay the money owed to creditors and seeks to have debts nullified through legal measures.
Collection account: a credit account that has not been paid in several months and thus been handed over to a collections agency.
Charged off: a debt written off by the creditor because the company has given up on getting the money from the debtor.

Credit bureau: an organization that collects data regarding an individual's credit transactions and provides it to financial institutions.
Credit record/ report: a detailed history of all your credit transactions and dealings with creditors.
Credit score: a grade you receive indicating your financial performance in relation to debt.
Creditor/ lender/ lending institution: the company you owe money to after taking out a loan or using a credit card.
Debt: something you borrow and need to give back; usually it refers to money owed.
FICO: a credit scoring model created by the Fair Isaac Corporation.
Foreclosure: the process by which a lender repossesses an item purchased on credit because a person no longer makes loan repayments, and the lender then sells the item to recover the remainder of the loan amount.
Garnishment/ garnishee order: a court order whereby an employer must deduct an amount from an employee's wages until debts are paid completely or alternative arrangements are made to pay the debt.
Hard inquiry/ hard pull: a credit score or credit report inquiry by a financial institution, usually after a person applies for some form of credit.
Installment: a set amount of money a person must pay infrequent intervals (usually monthly) until the full debt is paid, usually relating to large assets such as houses or vehicles.
Interest: a percentage added to the amount you owe, which the lender charges as a payment for the lending service.

Mortgage: usually refers to a home loan; a legal agreement between a person and a creditor to loan money with a physical asset (house) as security in case of non-payment.

Public filing: a judgment given against a person by the court relating to a financial situation; for example, bankruptcy, liquidation, garnishment, and so forth.

Revolving credit: a credit amount that becomes available as a person pays off their debts.

Security: something a person puts up to ensure a loan can be repaid in the case of payments no longer occurring; typically, security would be something valuable like a house, vehicle, piece of art, or jewelry.

Soft pull/ soft inquiry: a credit score or credit report check done for informational purposes and not to obtain additional credit; usually done when checking your won credit score, or by creditors who already know you.

VantageScore: a credit scoring model created by credit bureaus.

15 Things to Know About Credit

Most people will require credit at some time in their lives. You may want to buy a house, finance a car, or need the money to pay for your studies. There are also times when you require credit for less significant reasons. Some event tickets can only be purchased with a credit card, and you need to own a credit card to rent a vehicle while on holiday. Regardless of your reason for using credit, here are ten things you should always remember about credit.

1. Credit does not equal cash

Just because a bank gives some funds to you does not mean that you can go on a spending spree. The money in a credit card or loan is not your money! You do not own that money and will need to pay the funds back at some point in time. Be very careful with credit card spending as it can quickly spiral out of control. You should only use your credit card for occasional expenses, and only when you know you'll be able to make the required payments by the expected date. It is not advised to use a credit card for daily expenses such as food since it can quickly ruin your budget.

2. Credit scores and credit records are not the same thing

The credit rating score is a number between 300 and 850 to indicate how well you manage your credit. A number above 700 is considered to be a good score. A credit record (or report) is a detailed document that shows your personal information, past and current credit transactions, any legal cases regarding your finances, and other data. Your credit record will play a role in the calculation of your credit score.

3. A good credit score and credit record is essential

A high credit score will help you in your current financial situation and in the future. Any credit application you make will be impacted by your credit history. A good history of timely payments and credit management provides a sense of security to the lending institution. Your credit score and credit record provide an indication of the type of person you are when dealing with financial obligations. A good credit score has many benefits.

4. Five factors affect your credit score

The most used credit scoring model is FICO, which was created by the Fair Isaac Corporation. The FICO model considers five factors when calculating your credit score. A weighting is applied to each factor depending on its importance. The five factors are payment history, amounts owed to lenders, length of credit history, recent credit and applications, and your credit variety.

5. It takes time to build good credit

Credit history is not built overnight and you need to be patient. It takes at least 6 months to get a credit score, and that will be the benchmark from which to work. Your credit score is dynamic and will change over time. Thus, your credit score will also change as your responsibilities do. Most people take at least two years to establish a solid, good credit history.

6. Credit is not one-size-fits-all

Credit is not a universal item that can fit everyone. What works for one person will not necessarily work for another person. This reasoning is what makes a credit score and record necessary. A person who handles credit well should be rewarded for his actions; a person who goes into debt and does not make repayments should face the consequences. You may be able to compare your credit score with another person's credit score, but there are many hidden factors in your credit record that ultimately affect the credit you are offered from banks.

7. Anyone can get in trouble

Money is required in most transactions and sometimes things get out of hand. You may be managing your money just fine and then suddenly you have a pile of bills stacking up on your desk. Sometimes this happens because of a person's poor choices and irresponsible spending. Other times it is simply due to unforeseen circumstances. You should watch your finances very carefully and keep track of your credit so that you don't get into unnecessary trouble.

8. Businesses tattle-tale on you

Financial institutions, retail stores, gyms, and even libraries will keep a record of your transactions. The account information is shared by businesses with credit bureaus. This information will land up on your credit record and impact your credit score.

9. Checking your credit record is important... And free

You won't know what is reflected in your credit record if you don't check it often. Every person can get one free credit report per year from the credit bureau. You can use the record to check for any mistakes and identify areas to improve your credit score.

10. Paying bills is not enough

A credit record isn't just about paying bills on time. Other factors also play a role in your credit score. Paying your bills when due is important, but you need to take additional actions to decrease the amounts you owe and avoid interest. If you pay bills late it will be reflected on your credit record and affect your credit negatively. So simply making payments (on time or late) will not automatically give you a good credit score.

11. You can negotiate and save

A high credit score puts you at an advantage. You can negotiate lower interest rates and reduced security deposits with creditors. Lower financing costs will amount to masses of savings over the long term. Thus, credit can help you to save money that you can use for other things.

12. There is too much credit too

Some credit is good but it can quickly spiral out of control. Too many credit cards and big loans can make it difficult to meet all your financial obligations. You should keep your budget in mind and be able to pay back your monthly debts.

13. Never close an old credit card

The credit card you got first is one of the most important ones to hold onto. This account will give the most weight to the length of time for which you have had credit. Longer credit history is an advantage that you don't want to lose. Closing your oldest credit card can decrease the age of your credit and subsequently affect your credit score negatively.

14. Other factors affect credit applications

A credit score and credit record will affect any application you put in for additional financing such as home loans. Your credit application uses your credit record and other factors to determine your eligibility. Factors such as your income, age, and expenses will play a role in your credit approval.

15. There are no shared credit scores

A credit score belongs to you as an individual. You cannot share a credit score with someone else. Some people have joint bank accounts, or cosigned a loan, but that only means both parties are responsible for making payments. Your credit score remains your own, however, the actions of the other person can affect your credit score.

What is a Good Credit Score?

The credit score is a number that is assigned to you that reflects how well you use credit. When you attended school you would receive a report card indicating your performance, or grades, in a specific subject. Your credit score works just like a report card. **A credit score is a grade you receive, which indicates your financial performance based on specific factors.**

Factors affecting your credit score include payment history, type of credit, age of accounts, the amount of debt you have, and credit applications. These factors are explained in more detail in a later chapter. Another term you will see often in this book is credit record. A credit record is a list of all the transactions you have made relating to credit. The credit record will inform the credit score; as the record changes, so will your credit score.

There are two models that are used for credit score calculations: FICO and VantageScore. These models are used by most of the lending institutions in the United States and elsewhere across the globe. Both credit scoring methods are improved as new information becomes available. Fico 9 and VantageScore 3.0 are the latest models being used by companies.

FICO was created by the Fair Isaac Corporation and the most popular credit scoring model across the globe. The company was born in 1956 and has a long history in the financial services sector. VantageScore is a competitor, which was launched in 2006 after being developed by prominent credit bureaus. TransUnion, Experian, and Equifax worked together to create VantageScore and continues with improvements.

Credit Score Ranges

Fico and VantageScore use a range in which your credit score will fall. Both ranges are from 300 to 850, where a higher score is always better. The ranges differ slightly based on where it places your credit score ranking. The following tables provide an idea of how you may score for each model. The impact your score may have on your financial situation is also shown.

FICO Ratings

The ratings given by FICO are shown below along with the corresponding scores.

Credit Score

300 – 579

580 – 669

670 – 739

740 – 799

800 – 850

Rating

Very poor

Fair

Good

Very Good

Exceptional

People with a credit score between 300 and 579 are said to have a very poor score; this does not mean that the person is financially poor. It is unlikely that these people will be approved for credit. If an application does succeed, then the applicant may need to pay a deposit or additional fee as security.

A fair score (580 – 699) indicates that a person has previously missed payments and does not have a good track record regarding credit. It is possible to improve this score through proper credit control and gain a better record. People with a good (670 – 739) credit score can easily obtain credit. Additionally, there is a very small chance for these individuals to suddenly start making poor credit decisions.

Most people want to be placed in the category of very good (740 – 799) or have a score of more than 800 to achieve the rating of exceptional. These individuals will be offered the best credit card deals from top lending companies. Another advantage of a high credit score is that you will be given low interest rates when borrowing money.

VantageScore Ratings

The VantageScore ratings are slightly different as seen in the following table.

Credit Score

300 – 499

500 – 600

601 – 660

661 – 780

781 – 850

Rating

Very poor

Poor

Fair

Good

Excellent

VantageScore has an evener distribution of scores across the range. Those with very poor scores (300 – 499) have almost no chance of being approved for credit. These people will find it difficult to get credit and struggle to improve the score.

People with a poor (500 – 600) score might get a small amount of credit from some institutions. However, the interest rates will not be good and some places may ask for security or large deposits to ensure that the company receives their money back. A better position would be a fair score of 601 to 660. Individuals with this rating will get credit more easily but still have some issues with interest rates being high.

A good credit score (661 – 780) will ensure that a person is approved for credit and receive competitive interest rates. VantageScore considers anything above 700 to be a great score and that number falls within a good rating. The best rating is excellent with scores between 781 and 850. These individuals will receive favorable interest rates and easily be approved for credit from some of the top lending companies.

Understanding Credit Scores

Your credit score has an impact on credit applications in the future so you want to get it as high as possible. A credit rating of good is the minimum you want to aim for if you want to easily be approved for credit and get advantageous interest rates. FICO and VantageScore both indicate that about two-thirds of Americans have a rating of good or better. This statistic shows promise for people who are attempting to build credit. It is not that difficult to do if you are careful with how you use your available credit.

An important aspect for some people is a minimum credit score. Technically, the minimum credit score a person can have is 300. You may often hear groups talking about a minimum credit score if you want to apply for an account or loan. The truth is that there's no such thing. You do not need to have a minimum credit score to apply for credit.

Mortgage providers (the companies providing credit for home loans) indicate that even people with low credit scores can apply for home loans. The biggest difference is that you may not get favorable terms and good interest rates if your credit score is poor. Many lending institutions require a minimum down payment of 10% and additional security if your credit score is below 580. In contrast, a credit score higher than 580 only necessitates a 3.5% down payment. This example clearly shows why a good credit score is better for people.

Business Credit Scores

Businesses have credit scores just like individuals but the ratings work in a slightly different manner. You may be operating a business and need to take out a loan or purchase a vehicle on finance for company purposes. It is important to understand the differences between good credit scores for business and that of individuals.

The major difference lies in the actual credit scores: business credit scores fall within a range of zero to 100. Similar rules still apply and the closer your business is to a score of 100, the better it will be for your credit applications. A higher score will provide an opportunity for the business to obtain more credit, give access to additional funding and show your company is in a good financial position. There are three main agencies reporting on business credit: Experian, Equifax, and Dun & Bradstreet. Each reporting agency has its own way of calculating a business credit score, which is explained in later chapters.

The business credit reporting bureaus provide slightly different ratings even though they all work on a 0 – 100 point basis. Dun & Bradstreet uses their scoring to indicate the possibility of late payment. Businesses with a score between 1 and 49 have a high risk of missing payments; businesses scoring between 50 and 79 pose a moderate risk; while companies that have the lowest risk are those that score more than 80.

The Experian score is broken down into more segments: high-risk businesses score 1 to 10; medium to high-risk score 11 – 25; medium risk is obtained by businesses with a score of 26 to 50. The segments then become slightly larger. Businesses scoring between 51 and 75 pose a low to medium risk for lenders, and the lowest risk is when a business has a score of 76 to 100.

Equifax works slightly differently. They have one rating system for payment history and another for the likelihood that your business will fail. This book will only look at the one relevant to payment history. Instead of describing the scores in terms of risk, Equifax gives a ranking based on how you pay or how late your payment is to your creditors. Paying your creditors as agreed gives a score of 90 – 100; if you pay in the 30 days following the due date then your score is 80 – 89. A score of 60 – 79 is attributed for payment 31 to 60 days after the due date. Paying creditors 61 to 90 days late will result in a 40 – 59 credit score; while a score of 20 – 39 is given for payment between days 91 and 120. Any business paying creditors more than 120 days after the due date receives a score between 1 and 19.

Business credit may seem like something unnecessary for some business owners but there are many reasons to keep your shop in good credit standing. The major reason is to protect your personal credit score. By having a good business credit score you will not need to pay business debts out of your personal savings. As soon as business debts get out of control, you may need to pay from private accounts and this is not a situation you want to be in as you put your individual credit score at risk.

Summary

A credit score helps lending institutions to determine how well you manage your debts based on specific factors. The FICO model and the VantageScore model are commonly used to determine credit scores. Both models attribute a percentage of your credit score to factors that explain how you use your available credit. FICO considers a score of over 740 to be a good score, while VantageScore views a score above 700 as a good score. The credit score reported by FICO and VantageScore will always fall in a range between 300 and 850.

Businesses also have credit scores but these range from 0 to 100. The same rule applies – a higher score is better. The credit scores for businesses relate more to payment behavior than other factors. Businesses must ensure all payments are made on time as late payments directly affect the credit score. In some cases, there may be a link between the business credit score and an individual credit score, especially when debts start getting out of control.

The Benefits of a Good Credit Score

A person with a bad credit score can still obtain credit but may feel the consequences are too much. A poor credit score will result in high-interest rates that can quickly become expensive, especially if you take longer to pay your accounts. A good, excellent, or exceptional credit score will reduce the interest charges and help you to save money in the long run. There are many other benefits to having a good credit score.

Lower Interest Rates

Any person who has credit will need to pay interest on the outstanding account balance. The amount you borrow is often referred to as the capital balance. The balance outstanding is equal to the interest charges and the capital balance together. You can see interest as the profit the lending company gets for giving you credit; some places call it a financing cost. It is a fee that is levied every month in proportion to the amount of credit you have used and not yet paid back. A poor credit score will result in a higher interest rate and thus having to pay more fees. The advantage of a good credit score is a lower interest rate and pay fewer fees.

The lower interest cost makes it easier to pay back your capital balance. Most people are only paying back interest and then have the interest charged again on a monthly basis, which results in a vicious circle of only paying the interest. If you are only paying interest then it is difficult to pay back the capital balance you have borrowed. The better credit score and result in a lower interest rate can work to your advantage. It makes it possible to pay both interest and capital balance and in that way reduce your total debt.

Negotiating Possibilities

A high credit score provides leverage for negotiation. Your bank may have offered you a credit card with a set interest rate. You can approach other financial institutions and find out if they can give you a more favorable interest rate. This negotiating power helps you to find the best possible interest rate and offers with the lowest costs.

Having assets in your name will give you even more negotiating power. Lenders will always choose a customer who has security when it comes to providing credit facilities. Owning an apartment, vehicle, or other assets will give banks the knowledge that you can pay them back. Stable assets help in negotiations with financial institutions for decreasing interest rates and down payments. You should be proud of your high credit score and can always use it as leverage. Many people are scared to negotiate, but it can save you a bucket load of money in the long run. For example, an interest rate that is just 1% lower than the original quoted rate can reduce your total repayment with thousands of dollars. This money could be used in so many other ways than paying off a mortgage.

Improved Chance of Credit Approval

A better credit score makes it easier to be approved for further credit in the future. Every time you apply for credit, the financial institution will do a credit check. Your credit score is then made available to the company that made the request. The credit score will be used to help make a decision on whether the account should be opened, a credit card is issued, or a loan application approved.

Most people with a high credit score will qualify for a home loan or already have a home loan. Ensuring you make frequent payments on your mortgage can greatly contribute to a higher credit score, which will bring additional benefits. If you ever get to a point where you want to do renovations or need additional money, you can visit your home loan company and ask to refinance your home. This means that you will have funds made available to you but your mortgage will increase. You can still negotiate for good interest rates and lower fees. Plus, your longstanding relationship with the lender makes it easier to approach them for additional financing.

Great Credit Card Offers

Financial institutions want to work with customers who pay their bills every month. Your credit score is one of the things that is appealing to banks. Many banks will pull credit score information to find potential clients. The bank will then contact you and offer you some great credit card deals. Your own bank is also likely to provide you with better credit terms. If you get a call from a financial institution offering to provide you with a beneficial credit card, then you are most likely doing a great job with keeping your credit score high. Listen to the offer and ask the contact person to send you more information via email. You can then review the options and decide if this credit card is a good idea.

A solid credit score will lead to offers of credit cards with good rewards and other benefits. Some lenders will provide a credit card account to you without charging any monthly fees. Other institutions have rewards programs linked to the credit card. Using your credit card responsibly and for certain transactions will give you points or a specific reward's level. A higher score will qualify you for more rewards. The rewards can include reduced prices on airplane tickets or discounted rates on accommodation. Some financial institutions will add extra insurance cover, roadside assistance, or a personal banker to take your calls at any time of the day.

Better Insurance Rates

Car insurance is very important to protect you in the case of an accident, whether it is your fault or not. Automotive insurers look closely at credit scores when determining insurance premiums. The same goes for home owner's insurance. You need to have insurance to cover costs should your property ever sustain any damage. A person with a low credit score is perceived to be a high-risk client. The insurance company assumes that these people are more likely to claim from the insurance for unnecessary or fraudulent claims. This lack of trust results in higher insurance premiums.

A similar concept to the credit score is an insurance score used in some companies. The scores are not exactly the same but the general principle of a higher score is better stays the same. Your credit score will greatly influence your insurance score. People with a high credit score are seen as more trustworthy by the insurance companies. They benefit from lower insurance premiums thanks to a good credit record. Additionally, insurance claims may be paid more easily if you are in an accident or have damage to your home. After a claim, your insurance provider may increase the monthly premium to help cover some additional costs and to decrease risk. A higher credit score can be used to help negotiate a lower premium. Always ask your insurance provider to take your credit record into consideration when calculating your monthly premiums and excess amounts.

Better Rental Agreements

Landlords who rent out the property are always concerned about receiving their rental income. Many times a landlord will advertise an apartment but they don't know the people who eventually rent from them. Your credit score is one way for the landlord to learn more about prospective tenants. The landlord or rental agency will often use your credit report to see if you pay on time or miss payments. Oftentimes, landlords are more willing to let property to people with a high credit score and will outrightly reject applicants with a low credit score. A person with a good credit score is more likely to be approved for renting property since the landlord knows that the person is likely to pay.

Landlords are more open to working with people who have a high credit score, which makes the rental relationship much easier. For example, a person with a high credit score may be able to negotiate for a lower security deposit, or even have the possibility of paying the security deposit over a two-month period rather than paying the full amount at once. On the flip side, a person with a low credit score will most likely be asked to pay a substantially higher security deposit.

Fewer Security Deposits

A security deposit is often requested by companies as it shows that you will pay your account in the future. If you do not make payments, then the credit provider can use the security deposit to recover some of the costs. Security deposits are used by companies that provide both products and services.

Cellphone companies often require a security deposit since the customer gets the phone before full payment has been received by the company. This situation is very risky for cellphone providers. The security deposit can cover some of the costs if a person stops paying their cellphone account. Other companies that may require a security deposit are those which offer utilities, such as gas and water. A person with a high credit score often has the benefit of not paying a security deposit or paying significantly less. Your credit history and credit score have proven that you pay your bills on time and provides peace of mind for the company.

Self-Confidence

One of the biggest benefits of a good credit score is the boost your self-confidence experiences. You should be proud of yourself for saving your money and using your credit wisely. A good credit score takes time and effort to achieve. Achieving a high rating deserves a pat on the back. You also know that you can easily use your finances responsibly in the future.

Benefits of Good Business Credit

Businesses also benefit from having a good credit score. The most prolific benefit is the ability to get a loan more easily if your business has a high credit score. Your company will **receive loans quickly** and without much effort. A high business credit score will allow you to **negotiate favorable terms** with the lending company. These terms may include longer repayment terms and lower interest rates.

A good business credit score will **protect your personal finances** too since the company can rely on its own financial standing. Separation of business and person is vital for both parties to have a good credit record. A business that has a good credit score can get access to additional cash, such as an overdraft or business credit card. These resources prevent you from using your personal money to finance business expenses.

Loans are often crucial for **business expansion**, which is where a high business credit score can be particularly useful for your company. Talk to your local bank or a financial advisor to determine the best solution for you. Once your business has secured a loan or overdraft, you can use the funds to purchase additional equipment, stock, or do building renovations. The increased capacity of your business allows you to take in more work and potentially increase your income.

Prospective suppliers will consider your credit score when determining repayment terms. Many suppliers require businesses to pay cash on delivery for a period of time before opening a credit account to the business. Your company may be able to skip this step if it has a good credit score. The supplier may give you **more favorable terms**, including a three, six, or even twelve-month account for repayment.

Business credit cards offer similar rewards to personal credit cards, but you will only get these if the business has a good credit score. Most of the rewards for business will be in the form of a **cashback percentage** on the purchases made with the business credit card. You are effectively saving money with every purchase. The business can often use the cashback to pay for **reduced flight fares**, which is highly beneficial if your employees need to travel for work.

Many banks will provide the option to get an **extended warranty on any equipment** that you purchase with the business credit card. This benefit gives you peace of mind that you have a warranty cover even when something breaks. You can use your essential equipment for a longer period of time and still have it repaired at reduced rates.

Some companies provide credit cards to employees for business expenses. A credit card can help to keep track of all their spending, which works much better than using cash. It is a more secure method of payment and you can easily identify any unnecessary expenses. Remember that you need to **track your expenses** and purchases of large items for accounting reasons. A business credit card will always help you to track your expenses as they appear on credit card statements. You only need to keep hold of those statements and can quickly see where you are spending the business' money.

Summary

A high credit score indicates you are a responsible user of money entrusted to you. You should be very happy with a good credit score and can give yourself a pat on the back for working hard to get to this point. There are many benefits to having a good credit score. A higher score will always provide its owner with additional advantages.

Some of the biggest benefits of a good credit score are qualifying for lower interest rates and the opportunity to negotiate with creditors. These factors can lead to major savings in the long term. People with good credit scores receive some of the best credit card deals and can easily qualify for additional credit. Insurance companies also provide decreased rates for individuals with a high credit score; while landlords are more willing to lease homes to people with a proven credit record. Additionally, the total security deposits required for various transactions will be lower for a person with a higher credit score.

Businesses benefit from good credit scores too. Business owners can negotiate better repayment terms, keep personal finances safe, and get longer credit terms from suppliers. Business credit cards provide rewards to the business, decrease travel costs, and aid in tracking expenses. There are so many benefits and opportunities if your business and personal credit scores are good. Always strive to get your credit score into the exceptional category if you want the best potential benefits.

Factors Affecting Your Credit Score

A good credit score should be your aim and you are probably reading this book to find out how you can improve your credit score. To gain a full understanding, you should know how your credit score is calculated. Only once you know more about the factors which affect your credit score will you realize which parts you need to focus on for improvements.

FICO Factors

FICO is the most popular credit score system used by companies. FICO makes use of five factors to determine your credit score. The factor is payment history, amounts owed, credit history, recent credit, and credit variety.

Payment History

Imagine your friend asks to borrow $100 from you. The first thing you wonder is whether you will get your money back. Your answer may depend on previous experience with the person asking to borrow the cash. You may feel comfortable lending money to your friend Joe (from the Introduction) because he has previously paid back the money he borrowed from you. But you might say no if it was your friend Peter who asks to borrow money because you previously had to beg him to pay the money back.

Credit providers see it the same way as you would with your friends – they consider whether they will receive their money back if they lend it to you. This payment history is one of the factors FICO will consider when calculating your credit score.

Payment history counts 35% of your credit score. Your payments made to previous creditors are the biggest contributor to your credit score. It shows if you can make repayments when creditors trust you with their money. Paying your bills on time is exceptionally important to your credit score. You should be paying the minimum amount required by each creditor every single month. If you pay late then it will decrease your score. The later you pay, the more troublesome it will be for your credit score.

When you pay late, the model will look at certain aspects to determine how badly the situation affects your credit score. The company will consider how long ago the payment was due; missing a payment by a few days is not as bad as missing it by 60 days. The amount you were supposed to pay will also be taken into consideration. Another issue is if you missed multiple payments instead of just one; this will reflect very poorly on your credit score.

Some creditors approach debt collectors or collections agencies to retrieve money from borrowers who are not paying. This situation will reflect badly on you and can be concerning to potential creditors. Other issues that creditors will look out for in your payment history are bankruptcies, debt settlements, garnishee orders, foreclosures, or other legal proceedings.

Creditors will look at how long ago you missed payments. Someone who missed payments during the last year is considered to be a bigger risk when lending money. A person who missed payments several years ago but has been paying on time since will not be seen as having a large risk factor. Your credit score will also improve as time passes since the missed payment. You should not skip payments frequently but strive to pay every single installment as it becomes due. Late payments are usually erased once 7 years have passed since the missed payment.

Sadly, some people land up in trouble from poor financial choices or unfortunate circumstances. This situation can lead to lawsuits or forcing you to be declared bankrupt. These actions are known as public record filings and have dire consequences for people. Bankruptcies will have a negative impact on your credit score and remain on your credit report for 10 years. There are many legal factors to consider in this case and you may need to build up your credit from scratch with certain legal findings.

Amounts Owed

The next think creditors will look at is the amounts you currently owe to money lenders. They do not just consider this amount in isolation but also look at how much credit you have available from lenders.

A **credit utilization ratio** is an important number in this case. The ratio describes the percentage of the money you owe in relation to the total amount of credit you have available. For example, if you have $1,000 available on your credit card and you owe $250 for a purchase you made using the credit card, then your credit utilization ratio would be 25%. Most advisors consider a ratio of 10 – 30% as a good credit utilization level.

Amounts owed and the credit utilization ratio contributes 30% to your credit score. You may think that it is best to not owe any money but this is not the case. It is best to owe a small amount and show you are making monthly payments to reduce the balance. The repayments show financial stability and that you are responsible.

Another thing to remember is that the ratio will consider all of your credit streams. You may owe nothing on your credit card but recently took out a home loan. The different types of credit will affect your credit utilization ratio and the amounts owed must be seen respective to the type of debt. All types of credit accounts will be used for the credit utilization ratio. These will include credit cards, car financing, home loans, student loans, and store accounts.

Credit Length History

The length of time for which you have had credit plays a role in your credit score. It provides an idea of how long you have been using credit responsibly. Creditors will consider the age of your oldest account and the average age when you combine all the credit streams.

The duration for which you have been using credit will count 15% of your credit score. A longer period can be good if you have paid accounts on time. However, shorter periods are still okay but then you need to score high on the other factors.

There are three things that are used in calculating your credit history length. The first is the time which has passed since you received your very first credit agreement; for most people this would be a credit card or student loan. The second item to be considered is the length of time that other accounts in your name have been open. The final thing to remember is that the duration for which you have actively used your accounts will be factored into the calculation.

Financial advisors will often recommend you keep accounts open even if you no longer use the credit from those accounts. Your oldest accounts will carry a lot of weight on your credit score. Closing them can be detrimental and even decrease your credit score. Keep in mind that banks may decide to close an account on your behalf if the balance is zero for an extended time. Your account needs to have some type of balance to remain open. Even a small positive balance will be a great addition to your credit score.

Recent Credit

Establishing new credit will be another factor for your FICO credit score. Creditors will determine when last you applied for credit facilities and check the date your most recent account was opened. It is not a good idea to open too many accounts in a short period of time as it gives an image of desperation.

Many people try to open new accounts when they experience problems with cash flow. It causes them to take on additional debt even though they cannot afford to repay the funds. This situation greatly increases the credit utilization ratio. At the same time, it causes many creditors to do credit checks on your account. Even if you decide against taking out additional credit, the score calculator assumes you have opened more accounts, which can decrease your credit score for a short time.

Applying for new credit contributes to 10% of your credit score. When creditors do the checks it is called a hard inquiry. FICO saves hard inquiries done in the previous 12 months so you need to limit the amount of credit you apply for and the opening of accounts in any year.

The exception is vehicle and home inquiries. The company knows that it is unlikely for a person to purchase several vehicles and homes in a single year. Thus, FICO sees those inquiries as evaluations for interest rates and will see them as a single inquiry even if many companies check your credit record.

Credit Variety

The final factor for the FICO credit score is credit variety. FICO wants people to have all types of credit as it shows diversity in repayments. Credit cards and overdrafts are credit facilities provided by banks. You may also have a car or home loan, which is another type of credit. Accounts at stores or personal loans are yet a different credit stream.

In general, the model considers two types of credit. The first type is secured credit, and the second is unsecured credit. Secured credit takes place when you are paying for a physical asset such as a vehicle or house. If you stop paying those accounts, then the lender may eventually repossess the property to recover outstanding costs. Unsecured credit includes items such as short term loans, credit cards, and store accounts. These accounts do not have any physical property that can be taken back if you default on payments.

The variety of credit to your disposal forms 10% of your credit score. Try to have a good mixture of credit but don't worry if you do not have all the available types. It can harm your score if you suddenly apply for all types of credit. Most people will gradually build up their credit streams as their credit score improves through the years.

VantageScore Factors

VantageScore is very similar to FICO but has slightly different factors and weightings. The factors for VantageScore include your payment history, type and age of credit, percentage of credit limit used, recent credit actions and inquiries, and available credit.

Payment History

Payment history is once again the most important factor in the calculation of the credit score. Paying accounts late is a huge problem and VantageScore places emphasis on timely payments. The factor considers several years of payment history.

Payment history will count 40% of the credit score. VantageScore focuses on every payment being on time and late payments will have a negative effect on your credit score. The one big difference is that VantageScore considers mortgage payments as highly important. Missing your mortgage payment will greatly decrease your credit score.

Type and Age of Credit

Various credit streams are important to VantageScore. The company attributes a higher score to you if you have diverse types of credit. This is not always possible from the beginning but you may be able to build up credit facilities as time passes.

Credit streams and age of accounts contribute 21% to the credit score. You need to have many types of credit as you get older. The age of your credit accounts will also play a role. Do not close your earliest accounts. Keeping them open will improve your score.

Percentage of Credit Limit Used

The percentage of your credit limit used describes how much money if you have borrowed in relation to your credit limits. This is where the credit utilization ratio will come into play. Remember that you want to keep this percentage as low as possible but it should not be zero.

The percentage of credit you have used makes up 20% of the credit score. This factor counts almost as much as the previous one and it is important that you pay it enough attention. Keep in mind that the average will be taken for the credit utilization ratio and that the accounts will not necessarily be seen in isolation. The percentage of your credit limit you have used is also referred to as the debt utilization ratio.

Total balances and debt

Another factor that VantageScore considers is the total amounts you have outstanding. The amount you owe to any creditor is called the balance. On your monthly statements from the bank and creditors, it will show a balance at the beginning and end of the month, as well as a balance outstanding.

The total balances of credit will count 11% of your credit score. It is important to look at the balances outstanding to help you determine if you can pay back the debts owed. For example, you want to maintain balances on credit cards and store accounts at amounts lower than your salary.

This factor is crucial for every person to maintain good financial standing. You should have a good management on your finances, especially the amounts you owe to lenders. Your creditors will send you a statement every month with updated information and the outstanding balance. The balance should be well known to you and you need to keep those amounts in the back of your mind at all times. Add your debts together every month to know how much you owe in total. It will also help you stay on top of your total debts and you will quickly realize when your debts are starting to get out of control.

Recent Credit Actions and Inquiries

Any new credit you have taken on or any credit inquiries by potential creditors will affect your VantageScore. Every credit inquiry can potentially decrease your credit score so you need to keep it new account applications to a minimum. Many financial advisors suggest that you only open one account in any 12 month period.

Recent credit behavior and credit inquiries are allocated 5% of the credit score. It is not a lot but this is 5% of the credit score which you can easily maintain by not attempting to open several accounts at one time. VantageScore does keep in mind that home loan applications and vehicle financing may result in more than one check but gives a much shorter amount of time for these checks. Letting too many days pass between different company inquiries can lead to a decrease in your credit score. In most cases, credit inquiries for home loans or vehicle financing should be completed within a period of 14 working days, but at a maximum, it should take one calendar month. Any longer time period will reflect badly on your credit score.

Available Credit

The final factor considers the credit you have available. The amount of credit to your disposal will be taken into account for this factor. For example, if your credit card has a limit of $1,000 and you have used $200, then your available credit is $800.

Credit available to you amounts to 3% of the credit score. Available credit counts the least of all the factors for VantageScore but don't let this fool you. Other factors, such as the percentage of credit limit used, consider the other side of the coin. You want to have a good amount of credit available to get a great score for this factor.

Business Credit Score Calculations

Business credit scores are calculated in an entirely different way. The companies that calculate business credit scores are Dunn & Bradstreet, Equifax, and Experian. There are other companies but these three are most prevalent. Your credit score will range from 0 to 100.

The most important scoring factor is your payment history and the age of your credit history. In essence, business credit scores want to know two things. Firstly, does your company pay all its bills as they become due? And secondly, how long does it take your company to pay its bills? These two factors are extremely important since your business credit score is mostly calculated on your payment dates. Paying early or on time will give you a score closer to 100, but your score will quickly decrease with every 30 days a payment is late. Your creditors are also likely to report your business as a late payer even if you have only missed a due date with a few days.

Some business credit scoring models also consider risk in calculating a score. These models will usually provide you with two scores. The first score will be linked to your payment history, while the second score will consider how likely your business is to succeed. Companies with a lot of risks, little capital, or those in volatile industries may be said to have a high chance of failure. This score is sometimes referred to as a delinquency score. Financial institutions will keep this in mind when considering a credit application. Your industry may be a too high risk even if your business has an excellent payment history.

Summary

Two credit scoring models are used by financial institutions. The first is FICO, which is an acronym for the Fair Isaac Corporation and is the most popular credit score model. The second model is VantageScore, which was created by the credit bureaus Experian, Equifax, and TransUnion. Each model has its own factors that add up to a credit score or every person. The factors used in the calculations are very similar but each model does have its own unique characteristics.

FICO places most of its emphasis on your payment history and the amounts you owe to lenders. Your credit history (time period), and any recent credit inquiries are brought into consideration. Finally, FICO looks at the diversity of your credit accounts. VantageScore also places emphasis on your history of credit payments. Another key factor for VantageScore is the types of credit available and the age of your accounts. The percentage of credit you have used and your total debts are factored into the calculation. The final elements of VantageScore include any recent credit inquiries and the credit you have available to use.

Both FICO and VantageScore are credit scoring method used prolifically by financial institutions worldwide. The basis for calculating credit scores is heavily dependent on your payment history, type of credit, and age of credit. A crucial element to keep in mind is the credit utilization ratio. You should remember the factors affecting your credit score since they can help you to identify areas for improvement.

Business scoring models have payment history as its main factor contributing to a credit score. A risk factor, or delinquency score, will also be applied to businesses. A high score in a single category does not mean the other score will be high too, thus businesses should carefully consider any credit applications.

Checking Your Credit Record and Score

How do you improve your credit score if you do not know where you rate? The simple answer is to check your credit score frequently. Most financial advisors suggest checking your score at least once per year. Knowing what your credit score makes it easier for you to improve it, especially since some checks will provide you with the underlying credit record. Inspect the credit record carefully for any discrepancies or strange entries that may be incorrect.

Checking your own credit score is referred to as a **soft pull**. It means that you are just doing a check for your own information; the check is not to apply for new credit. Soft pull checks do not have an impact on your credit score. Your score will not increase or decrease when you do a check, but it will give you crucial information to use in the future.

A financial institution will check your credit score at times when you apply for a loan, overdraft, or new credit card. This type of credit check is referred to as a **hard pull** or hard inquiry. The checks done by lenders are comprehensive and they retrieve a lot of information about your credit dealings. The information is then used to evaluate your credit application and a decision will be made to approve or decline your request.

The three credit bureaus maintain your credit information used in your credit record. The credit bureaus are Equifax, Experian, and TransUnion. Each of these organizations gives you one free credit check per year. After that, you will need to pay a fee for additional records required throughout the year. You can request an online copy of your credit record or have it sent by mail. Keep in mind that some of the credit bureaus may charge a fee for sending the credit report by mail physical. The following table provides the relevant details for each credit bureau.

	Equifax	Experian	TransUnion
Website	www.equifax.com	www.experian.com	www.transunion.com
Mailing Address	Equifax Information Services, LLC Disclosure Department PO Box 740241 Atlanta, GA 30374	Download form on the website and send information to the relevant mailing address	Download form from the website and send information to the relevant mailing address

| Contact Number | 1-800-685-1111 | 888-397-3742 | 1-877-322-8228 |

The credit record will reflect specific information that can be divided into 4 segments. The first section contains **information about your identity**, such as your name, surname, and social security number. Check this information carefully for spelling errors or other mistakes. Lending institutions often make mistakes when reporting information to credit bureaus but this will not be a huge issue. Your residential address, employer's details, and spouse's information may also be recorded in the information section. Upon your request, you can have a personal statement added to your personal information section. The statement usually explains some entries on your report, for example, a shared bank account that has been closed.

The second section contains your **credit history**. All accounts will be listed along with the creditor's name and account number. Other credit history information reflected will include the account opening date, type of credit, whether it is an individual or shared account, loan amount, debt owing, and payment behavior. The credit record will state the payment history in English or give a code, which is explained at the bottom of your credit record.

The third section describes **public records** against your name. This section is the one that should have no entries since an entry will show there has been court judgment against you. Any financial situation that ended up in court will be displayed in this section. This information may be bankruptcy, tax liens, foreclosure, divorce judgments, or garnishee orders.

The last section of your credit record will indicate any **inquiries**. Every person or company who requested your credit record will be listed in this section. This part of the credit record will usually be divided into two parts to show both soft pull and hard inquiries. It is clear that a credit record contains quite a bit of information so take your time when you are checking your credit report.

Reasons to Check Your Credit Report

Checking your credit score will quickly give you an idea of how you rate on FICO or VantageScore. It will let you know whether you need to improve your score. The more important thing to investigate is the credit report. Your credit report will show all the transactions that affect your credit score. Looking at the report will help you to identify the areas in which you can improve your credit score. Here are some reasons to carefully review your credit record.

Rejected Credit Application

One of the major reasons to check your report is at times when someone denies your credit request. If you think that your credit score is good then it may come as a shock if you are not approved for a credit card or home loan. There is always a reason behind the rejection and you need to find out what the reason is as it could affect future applications.

Request a report from one of the three credit bureaus to see the reason. In most cases, a response on your credit application will be given in writing and mention which bureau was used for the check. You are then given 60 days from notification to pull a free credit report. The reason for the rejected application will be visible in the report. It might be that you currently have too much debt, or sometimes applications are turned down simply because a person does not have a good variety of credit.

Carefully check the report for any mistakes or questionable entries. For example, you may have paid an account in cash but the creditor did not record the transaction, which makes it seem as if you have missed a payment. You need to take this up with the creditor and have the error corrected to fix your credit score. Another issue is identity theft where someone uses your identity to get access to credit. You may not know about this situation until your credit application is rejected.

Identity Fraud and Theft

The concepts of identity theft and identity fraud are very close. Identity theft happens when a perpetrator steals a person's personal information. This information may include your bank account details, social security number, and passwords. Identity fraud occurs when the stolen information is used in various ways. In other words, the perpetrator is pretending to be you and using your accounts for various transactions.

Some people quickly pick up that they are victims of identity fraud. For example, if you check your bank statement frequently and you see a transaction that you know you did not make, then someone else may have access to your account. You can visit the bank to sort out the situation and may even receive some of your money back. But what happens when a criminal uses your information to take out a new loan or apply for a credit card? You may not know that this is happening and only realize the problem if your credit application is later denied.

Checking your credit report frequently will help you to identify transactions like credit card applications, which you know you did not make. You will then need to take it up with the authorities and relevant credit bureaus to get rectify the situation. If you don't, you are at high risk. The perpetrator can continue to use your information and can ruin your credit score. Oftentimes, the only way to know if your identity has been stolen is by pulling a credit report.

Preparing for a Loan Application

A good time to check your credit record is before applying for a new loan. It is best to check the score several weeks before you intend to apply for a car financing or a home loan. An early check will reveal what you can improve on your credit report and you can then get to work ironing out those issues.

Small outstanding amounts or mistakes on your credit record can have a big impact on your credit score. Settle any outstanding amounts, especially if they are late or if the amounts are very small. Any mistakes on your credit report should be rectified before proceeding with an application. If you know you want to buy a house next year, then now is a great time to check your credit score as you will have at least a year to improve it before applying for loans.

Surety and Cosigning Concerns

Sometimes a person needs a little help with their finances and you jump in to help. Your daughter may want to purchase her first car but since she just graduated and doesn't have a solid credit record, the bank is hesitant to finance the vehicle for her. The bank may be willing to provide a vehicle loan but she needs someone to cosign the loan. You agree to sign the contract with her but this means you are now also bound by the debt and your daughter's actions.

In this situation you have cosigned the loan; some lenders call this a surety signature. The two concepts are basically the same. In both cases, you agree to pay the debt in your personal capacity should the other person fail to pay. The cosigned loan will also appear on your credit record as you may be liable.

It is vital to check your credit record if you are acting as someone's surety. Pulling your credit record is the best way to check whether the person is making payments. If the other person has had late payments or stopped paying altogether, then it will decrease your credit score. It is better to check your credit report frequently and then talk to the other person about the late or missed payments. If the other person cannot pay you should go see the creditor to rectify the problem and make alternative payment arrangements.

It is clear that checking your credit report is important for many reasons. Doing a soft pull credit check is a prudent decision to help you keep track of your credit transactions. The record will help you to identify mistakes or raise red flags for identity fraud. Remember that checking your credit record is free so do it today!

Free Credit Checks

The most famous credit bureaus – Equifax, Experian, and TransUnion – allow individuals to do a free credit check once per year. You will need to request the credit report; it does not get sent to you automatically. Additionally, you must provide proof of identity to do the check. You can do a check more than once per year but then you will have to pay a small fee for subsequent credit reports. To do a credit check with these bureaus you will need to access **AnnualCreditReport.com**.

There are many companies across the globe that provides a free credit score checking service. These websites will usually say what model is being used, so check carefully if the credit score reported is based on VantageScore or Fico. Some companies have created their own models and may use an entirely different scoring method so you need to know how to evaluate your score.

Many of the websites which offer free credit score checks will have additional services. Some companies will ask you to sign up for an account and then update your score monthly so you can see your progress. The companies often mention which areas you have improved in and what factors need more work to increase your score. These checks are soft pull and will not have an impact on your credit score.

People who have **American Express** credit cards can see their FICO scores for free. Access your score through the online portal to keep track of your credit record. The score has a periodic update and you can see the FICO history for the previous year. American

Express uses credit information retrieved from Experian to report results.

Certain cardholders at the **Bank of America** can see FICO credit scores. The bank provides a monthly update based on data from TransUnion. Descriptive charts are also given to help you understand your credit score. One of the charts allows you to compare your score against the average scores of other users. You can get your free FICO report score from **Citibank** if you have a credit card with the bank. They will use your Equifax report and give a monthly update. People with a **Chase Slate** card can get a Fico score monthly, based on the Experian report.

Discover Bank offers free checks through the **Discover Credit Scorecard** program. All your checks are free and the system automatically updates your score every month. Most of the data come from Experian and the FICO model is used for this check. The best part is that you can use the service even if you are not a customer at the bank.

Walmart is one of the few retail companies which provide free credit score checks. The **Walmart MasterCard** and **Walmart Credit Card** are available via Synchrony bank and give you access to FICO checks. The catch is that you have to sign up to receive electronic statements.

Checking Business Credit Scores

Checking the credit score for your business is just as important as checking your personal score. The reasons for checking the score are very similar. The one difference is that some companies offer credit cards to their employees. You should carefully check your reports for any issues which may come up with employee credit cards.

There are several places to check your business credit score. Dun & Bradstreet offer free checks via **CreditSignal**. The website will let you know if there are any significant changes, which can also be tracked through a mobile application or the online dashboard. The service is limited though – you can get more advanced checks but only if you sign up for a subscription at an extra cost.

Another option is **Nav**, which uses information from both Dun & Bradstreet and Experian. Nav will give your credit score and summarized credit reports. You will need to pay for a full credit report if that is what you want to see. An extra feature provided by Nav is the ability to set goals to help you increase your score.

Free reports can also be received from **Scorely**, which shows you how to easily improve your score. The company provides the data and some tips if your business credit is getting out of hand. You can get a paid subscription if you feel you need even more help and resources.

There are only a few places that give a free business credit score; most companies require a fee to provide this information. Some websites will let you check your business credit report for free but it is only on a trial basis and you will not have access after a specified time period. You will usually get 7 or 30 working days for free and must then start to pay for the service.

Many businesses choose to pay for comprehensive credit reports as it is the only way to be certain of the facts. The three credit bureaus will charge you for your credit reports. Duns & Bradstreet use a D-U-N-S number and this service will require a payment of $159 per month but comes with many benefits. A credit report from Equifax costs $99.95 once-off. Experian offers a single CreditScore Report at $39.95, or a full credit report for $49.95.

Summary

A credit score gives an indication of how you handle your credit, but your credit record (or report) provides detailed information about your past and current credit situation. A credit report consists of four sections: identifying information, credit history, public filings, and inquiries. Checking your credit report is the first step to a better credit future and improved credit rating.

There are lots of reasons to check your credit score frequently. Some people check their credit records when a credit application is rejected unexpectedly. You do not want to fall victim to identity fraud and have money stolen – these types of transactions can be identified by inspecting your credit record. It is always good idea to carefully check your credit score before applying for loans. Another reason to check your credit record is to ensure any cosigned loans are being paid by the correct person. Checking your credit score and record allows you to identify any mistakes or issues before lasting damage is done. Everyone is entitled to one free credit per year from the three main credit bureaus. There are several websites you can visit to request a credit report. Another option is to ask for your report to be sent via physical mail but this action may incur a fee. Many of the websites are run by third parties who provide credit services. These companies offer a credit score update on a monthly basis so you can keep track of your credit actions.

Businesses should have a good idea of their credit record since it is mostly based on making timely payments. However, it's a good idea to review your business's credit record. You can request a credit record from several places but there are not as many options as with personal credit scores. Additionally, your business will usually need to pay to receive a business credit report. Many companies offer credit management services to businesses and will provide you with a monthly credit report and advice but charge a fee for these services.

Checking your personal and business credit score is a vital part of managing your finances. It is the first step to determining where you can improve your credit score. The credit record will help you in identifying any errors, and ultimately guide you in credit management decisions.

Building Credit When You Don't Have a Credit Record

Young adults and recently graduated high school students often face a dilemma when it comes to obtaining credit. You go to your local bank and apply for a credit card but after a stressful wait, the bank rejects your application. You call the bank to find out why the application was rejected and get told it is because you don't have a credit record. Okay, now you know you have to get a credit record, but how can you get a credit record? It is easy, simply get a credit card. This scenario has been the tumultuous experience of many young people. You need to have credit to get credit but it seems like an impossible thing to do.

Sometimes an adult doesn't have a credit score either. Some people prefer to work with cash, or maybe a stay-at-home partner who doesn't earn a set income. They will experience the same issue when applying for credit. Times change and you may need credit in the coming years for many reasons, which is why you now want to start building your credit score. You may want to purchase your first home, or need funds to pay for your child's tuition.

The problem with the credit score dilemma is not that you do not have money, the problem is that the bank has no proof you will pay back the money. Luckily, there are some ways to get around this situation and you do not always have to turn to the bank for help. Other lenders also present opportunities to obtain credit and build a credit record.

A first step before applying for credit is to check if any credit record exists for you. It may surprise you if you do have a credit record, especially when you did not apply for credit. Sometimes credit bureaus receive information from other places and this reflects on your credit history. For example, a gym membership that has a monthly debit order will reflect positively on your credit report; or you may have a mobile phone contract that deducts the contract fees at the end of each month. Even your landlord may be reporting your good monthly payments to the credit bureaus and you wouldn't even know it.

Another thing to remember is that credit history is only kept for a set amount of time – you need to use the credit given to you if you want to have a credit record. If you open an account but don't start to use it within the first six months then you will not have a credit record. This situation defeats the purposes of building a credit record. Try to use your credit card at least once a month to show you can also pay it back responsibly.

Remember: just because you don't have a credit record does not mean you have bad credit!

Getting Credit for the First Time

Now that you are ready to get credit, you will need to make it a reality. There are several places to approach and things to do in an attempt to secure your first credit. Try the banks, retail stores, or cosigning on an account.

One of the first places to visit is your **local bank**. If you have an existing account with a specific bank then go talk to an advisor on how you can obtain credit. Many banks are willing to help out with a credit card if they know your financial history from being a client for several years. Some banks will offer you a **student credit card** during your studies. These cards have a very small limit but are the perfect tool to establish a good credit record.

Retail stores offer **store accounts** to shoppers. You can use the store cards at the specific stores, but sometimes a host of companies will offer one card for several different stores. Keep in mind that you are getting a store account to improve your credit score.

The idea is definitely not to use your new credit to fund a shopping spree – the last thing you want is to owe money when you actually trying to build credit. The limits on store accounts vary and most first time users will get a small limit. However, the interest rates can be extremely high so determine what the best payment method will be before you start using the account. Find out from friends which retailers they have received accounts from since this will make it easier. Try a clothing store, food market, or other retailers who offer accounts. Many of the retailers will be satisfied with knowing just your income and expenses and will grant a store card based on these factors.

There are other financial institutions besides the bank that may grant you credit. Do a search of lenders in your area to find out which companies you can approach for a credit card. Some companies are willing to give you a credit card if you can put up security. For example, if you want a credit card with a $500 limit, then the lender will require a cash deposit of $500 or more to grant you the card. A **security deposit for a credit card** is usually only required once-off as a token of good faith. There are some different things to consider when using a secured credit card. The fees can be very high, which will be an extra charge, or even take money from your savings. The best option is to check the fees and interest rates with the credit card issuer. You need to also check that the lending institution will be reporting your credit information to the credit bureaus; otherwise, it defeats the purpose of getting the account in the first place.

You can also turn to your family to help you obtain credit. A family member may have a credit card or account and you can apply to be an **authorized user of the card**. The account remains in the family member's name but you can use a set limit and build credit in this way. Another method to get credit is to **ask a family member to cosign for your credit card**. A family member who cosigns is putting their own credit score at risk because if you miss a payment then it will reflect on their record. You should use this method if you know you are going to be able to pay your credit card. It is not fair to let your mistakes affect someone else's good credit standing. Take responsibility for your credit record and make all your payments on time.

One of the lesser-known methods to obtain credit is through a **credit-building loan**. These loans are only offered by a few lenders and the aim of this loan is to build a good credit score. You can apply for a credit-building loan of a suitable amount – let's say $2,000 – which the lending company will place into an account. You cannot use the $2,000 at any point in time but you need to pay a monthly installment on the loan. When you have paid the full amount of the loan, the lending company will deposit the money into your account. They will also inform the credit bureaus of how many payments you have made and whether you missed any payments. This type of loan is one of the best ways to secure a credit history and has the added benefit of making your cash available once the full payment has been made.

Any type of account that you pay on a monthly basis can help you to build your credit score. Think of accounts such as water, electricity, rent, or subscription services. All of these payments are made monthly and you are penalized if you pay late or miss a payment. It is a good idea to call the different service providers to find out if they send reports to the credit bureaus. If they do then you may already have a reasonable credit record. Alternatively, ask them to send through reports as it will help you build your credit history.

Responsible Credit Use

Getting your first credit card or credit score can be very exciting but you need to be careful. The early days have very few transactions and any misstep can lead to a poor credit rating. You must use your credit responsibly to ensure that you build your credit. Every transaction at the beginning of your credit history will play a role as you have few entries. You need to build up your credit score systematically and ensure every credit action reflects positively on your credit record.

Make all your **payments on time** and even earlier if possible. Do not let any account get behind. Set yourself a goal to **deposit a certain amount** into your credit card every month, even when it does not have an outstanding balance. This action shows you are committed to paying and you will actually earn interest income on a positive balance. If you are worried about forgetting payments, then you may want to consider an **automated payment** to ensure timely transactions. Your minimum payment amount will then be deducted from your transactional or savings account on a set date each month. You can always transfer additional funds to the credit account at other times to quickly decrease the amount you owe.

Store accounts should also be paid frequently. A small amount can be **paid off at the end of the month** or split a larger amount into three **monthly payments**. Some store accounts come with set terms and conditions, which you need to check. For example, many store accounts will provide you with 90-days interest-free credit. If you pay your account within 90 days of purchase, then you won't have any interest charges. Payment of the account after 90 days from purchase can lead to high-interest rates and will reflect badly on your credit score. Certain stores may require a minimum amount to be paid back every month so check the fine print for any such stipulations.

Always consider the factors that impact your credit score: payment history plays a large role, as well as the credit utilization ratio. New credit users should keep their **credit utilization ratio below 30%,** which means that you only use 30% of the credit you have available to you. Some financial advisors and credit bureaus feel new credit users must have an even lower number. Many suggest that a ratio of 10 – 20% reflects better on first-time credit applicants. Avoid excessive debt when you just start to borrow money to show you are using your credit responsibly.

A great way to ensure responsible credit usage is to decide on how much you can pay back each month before you even start applying for credit. Look at your current monthly budget and **determine your disposable income** at the end of a month. This amount should be what is left over after you have paid your rent, all your bills, purchased food and any other things you may require during the month. The amount remaining at the end of the month is usually what you can afford to pay towards credit accounts. Remember that you don't want to spend the full amount each month; you want to keep some of your disposable income for unexpected expenses, to put towards savings, or to treat yourself.

Another important thing is to **not apply for too many accounts**, even if you want to build your credit record. Every application will result in a credit check and this can greatly decrease your credit score if lending companies do checks often. You need to **limit new applications** to once every 6 months and then you should only apply for one card or loan. On the other hand, you don't need to have a whole bunch of cards at a young age because it can make you look desperate and in need of cash.

The best way to build your credit score is to open a secured credit card or a retail store account, and then follow up with another credit stream in the following year. Use your credit responsibly and you will see your credit score increasing with time. It takes about **six months for most people to build credit** into a good score. Part of the reason for this time period is that credit scores only start to take effect after credit accounts are open for at least six months, even if the lender already starts reporting credit actions after the first month. You will see your credit score changing every month once the first six months have passed, so use your credit carefully during the first few months as you want to start with as high a score as possible.

Building a good credit score is always easier than fixing it once it has sustained damage. Keep your credit score healthy by avoiding the **four pitfalls** to which many people fall prey. Firstly, avoid late payments at all costs as it will remain on your credit record for seven years. Secondly, people do not use their credit cards resulting in the account being closed, which means you have to start from scratch. The third pitfall is spending more money than you can afford to pay back. Finally, most people obtain credit but do not check their credit records for mistakes or fraudulent transactions. Avoiding these pitfalls will help you to stay in control of your credit score and your finances.

Summary

Obtaining credit for the first time can be a challenge since you don't have a credit history yet. You will need to start somewhere, and the best thing to do is to find out if you have a credit score. If you do then you have a starting point, but if you don't have a credit score then you will need to find a place willing to give you credit.

Visit your local bank to apply for a student credit card or a secured credit card. Alternatively, open a retail store account, become an authorized user on a family member's account, or open a credit-building loan. Another option is to ask someone to cosign for your credit card.

You should use your credit responsibly at all times to build a strong credit record and a good credit score. Make all your payments on time or automate payments for monthly account payments. Pay at least the minimum amount owed, but add extra if possible to avoid high-interest rates. Include your repayments in your budget, and ensure your credit utilization ratio is around 20%. Limit your new credit applications to one every six months, and check your credit score frequently for any changes. Once you have established your first credit, you should start to have more credit opportunities made available to you.

Maximizing Your Credit Score

The importance of a great score is irrefutable. Today is the day to start improving your credit score and get it as high as possible. The better your financial actions, the higher your credit score will become. There are many ways to improve your credit score but a strategy is always a good idea.

Once you have gotten your credit record you need to identify the factor where you are scoring the poorest. You also need to remember the weighting assigned to each factor when deciding on an improvement strategy. We will be looking at the FICO model specifically, but you can use the same strategy for VantageScore since the basic premise remains the same.

Remember the five main factors are:
- Payment history (35%)
- Amounts owed (30%)
- Length of credit history (15%)
- Types of credit (10%)
- New credit and inquiries (10%)

Let's see how each of these factors can be improved. Some strategies are quite easy and will be quick to implement. Other strategies may take longer to have an impact on your credit score.

Improving Your Payment History Weighting

Your payment history is the one thing you can fully control but it is also one of the most difficult factors to improve. As soon as 30 days pass since you miss a payment it will reflect on your credit report. The best way to maximize your score is to continuously **pay all your accounts on time**, including rent and other utilities. Missing just one payment will result in an entry on your credit report so it is best to avoid late payments altogether.

One option to help boost your payment history is to **pay larger sums** to your credit card and store accounts than the minimum required amount. For example, if you need to pay $200 monthly towards your credit card, but you receive a work bonus, then you can pay an additional amount towards the credit card. The result is that your overall amount owed decreases, less interest is charged, and thus a smaller premium is required to be paid in the following month. It makes it easier to then keep up with payments, even in months when your cash flow is running low.

A **credit-builder account** is another great way of building a good payment history score. A credit-builder account is initially a "loan account" that financial institutions have available. The lender will approve you for a set amount and give a payment period of 12 – 24 months. However, you will not get access to any money upfront. Instead, you pay a monthly installment to the loan account. Once the time period elapses you then have access to all your cash (you can see this as a savings account). The lender will report good payment history to the credit bureaus, which will help to improve your score.

Improving Your Amounts Owed Weighting

Your amounts owed weighting can be improved if you improve your credit utilization ratio. One way to do this is to **apply for a credit limit increase** on one of your credit cards. However, this doesn't mean you should use more of the available credit. For example, if you have a limit of $10,000 and you owe $4,500, then your credit utilization ratio is 45%. You ask the bank if they can increase your credit limit and approve a new limit of $15,000. You still owe $4,500 but the new credit utilization ratio is 30%. The lower credit utilization ratio is a positive event and will increase your credit score.

Improving Your Credit History Length Weighting

The average age of all your accredit accounts will be used to calculate your credit length. The first account you opened is the most important to maximize your score since it will increase the average age of credit. There is really just one way to maximize the weighting of credit history length and that is to **keep your first account open**. Many people make the mistake of closing their early accounts but this will decrease your score. If you do want to close an existing accounting then it is best to close your latest account or one you opened in the last two years.

Improving Your Credit Mix Weighting

Your credit mix or credit variety is one of the more difficult factors to improve. It requires you to open additional accounts or loans, which will increase your total credit available but decrease your score if too many inquiries are done at the same time. Many people also do not want more credit but may find it is difficult to improve their credit score without additional credit.

Generally speaking, there are two kinds of credit: revolving and installment. A revolving credit account has no set end date and you can use your own amount to spend. Revolving credit types typically include credit cards and store accounts. These accounts have a set limit but as long as you make payments, the credit continues to be available to you. Installment credit usually relates to accounts for which you have to pay a set amount each month. Examples include vehicle loans, mortgages (home loans), student loans, and personalized loans.

Advisors suggest that you should have a **minimum of one revolving account and one loan account**. This situation shows that you can handle different types of credit and can use both types responsibly. One of the main reasons to have a good mix is to ensure you are approved for larger credit transactions, such as purchasing a high-value car or permanent residence. Most people are able to get a credit card quite easily but struggle with obtaining a loan. One of the best ways to get a loan is to open a credit-building loan, as explained previously. Another option is to visit your usual bank and ask to open a small personal loan account. You can then pay off the installments each month to help build your credit score.

Improving Your New Credit and Inquiries Weighting

Getting **new credit** is a method to increase your credit score, for example, by applying for a new credit card. You should only do this if you have a relatively stable credit record, or if you haven't made an application in the last 6 months. An additional credit card or store account will affect several of the weighting factors. It will help to show you have new credit while keeping the number of inquiries low per year. You will also be increasing the types of credit that you have available. Another benefit is that your available credit will increase while your credit utilization ratio will decrease. Be careful though to not immediately spend an excessive amount on the credit card; rather, keep your balances low.

Increase Your Credit Score Quickly

There are several ways to improve your credit score in a quick and efficient manner. These changes are small things but will have quite a bit of impact on your credit score. Most lenders will only report your credit transactions once per month, so do not expect to see a difference in credit score overnight. Follow the next few steps to make fast changes to your credit score.

1. **Check your credit record**. Apply to get your full credit report from all three credit bureaus (Experian, Equifax, and TransUnion). You should also sign up for a website that provides a monthly credit score update – many provide a free service for just a basic score.
2. **Analyze the credit report**. Look for any mistakes or entries you know were not made by you. Also, check if all your credit accounts are being reported to help boost your score. Report any mistakes to the relevant credit bureau for correction. Rectifying the mistakes will change your credit score to be higher.
3. **Look for missed payments**. If you know you missed payments, or your credit report shows missed payments, then you need to pay the debts immediately. The longer you take to pay missed installments, the lower your credit score will become.
4. **Settle small debts**. Check if you have any accounts with small balances and pay them. If

you have a card with a small amount outstanding, then you can pay a bit extra so that the card has a positive balance.
5. **Create an action plan**. Develop a budget to help you have enough money for your monthly credit payments. Determine if you need to be paying more on your accounts, or consider opening another account to increase your credit variety.

The three credit bureaus only provide a free credit report once a year. However, there are many other companies who draw your information from the credit bureaus and then report your credit score. These companies often have a sign-up service, which will update your credit score every 30 days at no extra cost. You can use these services to check how your score improves as you make positive changes.

Summary

Maximizing your credit score should be a top priority if you want to access credit in the future. A high credit score shows you can use borrowed money responsibly, and that you take your finances seriously. There are a lot of different ways to increase your credit score, but first, you need to determine the areas of your credit score that can be doing better. Check your credit record for low scoring areas and determine a strategy from that point.

Your payment history score can be improved by paying your accounts on time, opening a credit-building account, or paying more than the minimum required amount. The amounts you owe are factored into your credit score, specifically using the credit utilization ratio. You can improve your credit utilization ratio by applying for a credit limit increase on your credit card but only do this if your credit is in good standing.

The lengths of time your accounts have been open are another key factor, which can easily be improved by keeping your oldest accounts open. Your credit mix score will be higher if you have different types of credit; try to have at least one installment (loan) account and one account with revolving credit.

Finally, limit your new credit inquiries to one per six months since it shows you are stable and not seeking credit desperately.

The increase your credit score will not happen overnight, but you can see systematic increases if you continuously use your credit in a responsible manner. By scrutinizing your credit record frequently, you will be able to identify any errors and find areas to improve. Settle small balances as quickly as possible, limit new credit inquiries and create action plans to take control of your credit situation. Following this advice will allow you to see changes in your credit score as time passes.

How to Avoid Things that Lower Your Credit Score

Now that you know how to get the most out of your credit score, let's consider some things that can lower your credit score. Some of these items are under your control, but some problems you may not even be aware of until it affects your life in a negative manner. Staying on top of your finances and checking your credit report often can help you to avoid these types of problems. There are several ways to avoid a decrease in your credit score. Avoiding a lower score requires vigilance and prudent financial management.

Millions of people suffer from a poor credit score because they do not realize there are mistakes on their credit record. This low score is simply due to ignorance and entirely unnecessary. The first step in sorting out your credit score is always to check your credit record. Go through it line after line and **check for any errors** on your credit report. Once you find any issues you will need to report it to the relevant credit bureau.

Sometimes the lending institutions do not update your details with the credit bureaus, which results in a lower than the anticipated score. For example, your credit card limit may have been increased but the bank has not yet informed the credit bureau. Request the bank to **correct this information** and it will help to increase your credit score.

Perusing your credit report for errors may also help you to identify entries that do not relate to your accounts. Oftentimes such entries are the result of **identity fraud** and someone else may be racking up accounts on your behalf. It is crucial that you sort out this situation before the criminal completely wrecks your credit score. Inform the credit bureaus of the suspected fraud, open a case at the relevant authorities and notify the relevant creditors about the problem. If the transactions are occurring on just one account then it is best to inform the lending institution and request that the account is frozen until the situation is sorted out. This temporary solution will prevent the thief from acquiring any further funds through a specific account. There is a faster way to identify fraudulent transactions: **request monthly statements for all your accounts** and thoroughly check them for strange transactions. In this way, you will know of the problem at the earliest possible time and may avoid lowering your credit score.

Another method to avoid lowering your credit score is to not pay accounts late. **Stay up to date** with all payments, and preferably make more than one payment per month on your credit card or store accounts. **Do not skip any payments** or installments as this can be detrimental to your credit record. Remember that you need to **budget** to have enough money available to pay all your credit accounts. First, put away all the money for your credit accounts before you start spending on frivolous items. **Do not transfer credit card balances** to other accounts to help you pay your bills – this can decrease your credit score and affect several factors poorly. Do not use one credit stream to pay for other credit types. It is best to ensure you have enough funds available to pay all your credit.

Remember that you should **never max out your credit cards**. This issue occurs when you use all the available credit on a specific credit card. The bank will not allow you to continue using the card until you pay enough money to negate the effects of interest. Maxing out your credit means you are increasing your total debt and increasing your credit utilization ratio. **Avoid high debt balances** if you want to improve your credit score. A responsible person does not have a credit utilization ratio of more than 50%;

people with good credit scores use less than 30% of their total available credit.

Avoid a decrease in your credit score by **timing your credit applications correctly**. Applying for new credit cards or store accounts should preferably only occur once every twelve months. Applications for home loans or vehicle financing often include rate checks from several different lenders; in this case, you should try to complete all applications within a 14-day period to avoid a score decrease. Many companies will provide some form of incentive for you to apply for credit. Be wary of any company that offers you a reward in return for your application since the credit check will be done but you might not be approved, which means your new credit inquiry factor could decrease your credit score. For example, you may have received a letter in the mail from a bank complete with a credit card glued to the inside of the letter. The letter will say you are pre-approved but a hard inquiry needs to be done before they can give final approval. It is best to cut up those cards and shred the letter. Another example is store cards: a salesperson will approach you while you are shopping in-store and offer you an account with great incentives. These incentives may include shopping vouchers or free merchandise, but only if the account is approved by the store.

Keep the age of your credit higher by leaving all credit accounts open. Never close your credit cards as it makes the average age lower. At the same time, you don't want too many open accounts as this can also decrease the average age of your credit. For example, if you have a credit card that is ten years old and open a new card now, then the average age of your credit would be five years, which will decrease your credit score. However, if you opened a credit card ten years ago and got another credit card five years later, then the average age would be 7,5 years. The average credit length is a difficult concept to work with since you need to have more credit to increase your credit score but at the same time, new accounts can also lead to a decrease in score. The best option if you want additional credit is to **apply for a credit limit increase** since it will have the least impact on your credit score.

You may be tempted to help someone else with obtaining credit and decide to co-sign a loan with the other person, but this is never a good idea. **Do not co-sign loans** as the other person's actions will impact your credit score. Sometimes you do not have a choice, such as with business loans or mortgages. In these cases, you should be extra vigilant to ensure your credit record is not affected by another person's poor choices.

Summary

The last thing you want is to lower your credit score. Unfortunately, some things can cause your score to decrease, even if they stem from unintended actions. Always check your credit record for errors or fraudulent entries as these are the items that can lower your credit score without your knowledge. Request the credit bureau and lending institution to correct the information on your credit record. Check your bank statements and credit record for fraudulent actions as it can be an indicator of identity fraud.

The best way to avoid credit score decreases is to keep payments up to date and never pay your accounts late. Keep abreast of your credit utilization ratio and do not let it go higher than 30%. Avoid high balances on your credit accounts and do not max out your credit card. Both of these status are detrimental to your credit score.

The timing of new credit applications should be done carefully, and never apply for more than one account in a six-month period. Do home loan applications in close succession to avoid lowering your credit score. Avoid co-signing loans or credit cards as you become responsible for another person's actions. Keeping your credit score high is not difficult; you just need to keep track of your credit record and make smart financial decisions.

Credit Score Myths

Myths… those little tales that creep into stories and distort reality, but often without holding any truth. There are many myths regarding credit scores and what goes into the calculation of a score. But sometimes people just start making assumptions about a credit store, hear something incorrectly, or have a misconception regarding their credit report. The bases of these myths often lie in mistaking your credit score with the requirements for a credit application. There are also general credit score myths, which will be taken into consideration.

Let's first review what we know about credit scores before we delve deeper into the myths. Two credit score models exist: FICO and VantageScore.

Factors affecting Credit Scores	
FICO • Payment history • Amounts owed • Credit length history • Recent credit • Credit variety	VantageScore • Payment history • Types and age of credit • Percentage of credit limit used • Total balances and debt • Recent credit actions and inquiries • Available credit

Always remember the factors which have an influence on your credit score as shown above. No other factors can influence your credit score. Still, there are several myths about what impacts your credit score. The myths perpetuate the idea that elements like gender, employment status, education, income level, and other things will affect your credit score. But this is simply not true. The best way to check if it is a myth is to refer back to the original factors. For example, nowhere in the factors does it say that your gender will affect your credit score; neither will your ethnicity.

Each of the myths will be considered in more detail and will explain if it may affect your credit application, but it will never affect your credit score. Other myths will be discussed too, which may lead to misconceptions regarding your credit score.

Myths about Demographics and Personal Characteristics

Myth: You will share a credit score with your spouse after you marry.

Truth: A credit score is linked to you as a person; to get a credit score you need a social security number (or identification number). Your identity is not lost when you get married; neither do you receive a shared social security number with marriage. Each person retains their own identity. However, you may decide to open joint accounts with your partner or co-sign for loans. Many couples decide to buy a house together and then share the responsibility of payment. Only joint accounts and co-signing agreements will have an effect on both spouses' credit scores. The accounts held in individual names will not impact on the other person's credit score. *Each person maintains their own credit score after marriage.*

Myth: Your credit score will be checked by an employer.

Truth: Your employer may not use your credit score to make employment decisions. Employers may check your credit report (but not your credit score) when your financial management plays a part in the specific job. You have to keep in mind that there is a difference between a credit record and a credit score. *Employers may check your credit record but not your credit score.*

Myth: A high bank balance improves your credit score.

Truth: The amount of money you have or your income will not affect your credit score. It can only impact your ability to pay back creditors but that is all. Your income level and bank balance are not part of the factors contributing to the final credit score. However, some lending institutions require you to have a good credit score and back-up finances to be approved for credit. Lenders will reject an application based on a good credit score alone; they must consider other factors. *A high bank balance may help you to be approved for additional credit.*

Myth: Your salary affects your credit score.

Truth: Your credit score is only a general reflection of how you handle your credit accounts and repayments. Remember that your salary is not included in the factors used to calculate your credit score. Lenders may use your salary to help decide whether you get approved for credit. Your salary helps to show creditors that you have enough money to make repayments. Other forms of income such as alimony or child support also do not form part of your credit score. *Salary is not a part of the credit score factors.*

Myths about New Credit

Myth: You need substantial debt to get a good credit score.

Truth: We have already seen that there is a dilemma when a person with no credit score needs to obtain credit. Luckily, you don't have to make a lot of debt to get a good credit score. Of course, your total available credit plays a role in your credit score. However, you can build a good credit score with only one credit card and ensure you pay it back often. Also, remember that rent and subscription services can be reported to the credit bureaus to help you build credit. *Paying off a small credit card balance will help in getting a good credit score.*

Myth: No debt means your credit score is good.
Truth: Having no debt means you haven't yet opened a credit card, store account, or loan. It also means that you usually use cash to do transactions and have no formal debt. On the other hand, you may have had a lot of debt and subsequently paid it all back, but if your credit score was poor to start with, it still may be. Bankruptcy can also create no debt but this situation is detrimental to your credit score. Your credit history will always play a part in your credit score, even if you do not currently have any debts. *Your credit history affects your credit score.*

Myth: You won't get any credit if you have a bad credit score.
Truth: Lending institutions do not approve credit based only on your credit score. Several other factors play a role in credit approval. For example, your total debt and monthly income will impact on the credit application. So your credit score might be low but you still have the possibility of getting credit. The only issue with being approved while having bad credit is that there will be more terms and conditions. Higher interest rates are usually applied to people with poor credit scores and you may be required to pay a sizeable security deposit to obtain the credit. *You can get credit subject to certain limitations even if you have a bad credit score.*

Myth: A bankrupt person gets a new credit score.
Truth: When people file for bankruptcy, they are admitting that they can no longer pay back their debts. There are many reasons for this happening,

which may include poor financial decisions, acquiring credit due to unforeseen circumstances, or losing their jobs and no longer having an income. A person can only be declared bankrupt by a court after providing various documents to support their claims of no longer having enough money to pay creditors. At this point, the person has already missed payments and amassed a ton of debt, which means the credit score will most likely be very low already. A bankrupt person will no longer have a credit score since they cannot go into debt after the bankruptcy filing for a certain period of time (7 to 10 years). *A bankrupt person's debts will be erased but the public filing will remain on the credit record.*

Myths about Credit Score Factors

Myth: An account dispute can improve your credit score.

Truth: Incorrect information on your credit record should be addressed with the relevant credit bureau. Checking your bank statements can also help to identify issues. Finding a mistake does not mean that it will definitely be erased from your credit record – lookout for the fine print when opening accounts. In many cases, the error will be corrected but it may not improve your credit score. *Your credit score won't increase if the corrected mistake contributes just a small percentage to your credit score.*

Myth: Your score improves when you close a credit card.

Truth: The average age of your credit accounts will decrease when you close a credit account. It also decreases your available credit, which will increase your credit utilization ratio. This situation can have a negative effect on your credit score. Some people close credit accounts while they still owe money on the account, which is an even worse thing to do. *Your credit score will increase as credit accounts become older if the accounts are in good condition.*

Myth: Your credit score will decrease if you check it often.

Truth: Checking your credit score is referred to as a soft pull. You are only checking it to look out for errors and to see your credit score. A credit score can only decrease if many lending institutions check your credit score in a short amount of time in the process of a credit application. *Doing a check for your own knowledge will not affect your credit score.*

Myth: Only check your credit score before a loan application.

Truth: Checking your credit score will help you to identify any problems on your credit record before they have a lasting impact. Your score may be too low if you only check it before a loan application. If you check it before then, you may identify issues and can correct them before applying for your loan. In fact, checking your credit score frequently gives you a benchmark for improvement. *Check your credit score and report at least once every year.*

Myths about Bad Credit

Myth: A bad credit score can only be improved after 7 years.

Truth: Missed payments and negative judgments will remain on your credit record for 7 years. However, there are other parts that can help you increase your credit score, like paying your accounts on time, maintaining credit diversity, and having a suitable credit utilization ratio. *Your credit score can improve quickly if debts are managed well and payments made on time.*

Myth: A poor credit score never goes away.

Truth: Your bad credit score will remain on your record if you keep on making poor financial decisions. Continuously missing payments, a high credit utilization ratio, and maxing out credit cards will always affect your credit score. However, once you start to make sound financial decisions and pay creditors on time, your credit score will slowly start to increase as time passes. *Improve a bad credit score by making good credit decisions.*

Myth: A credit score will only become worse after a long period of time.

Truth: Do not be mistaken by thinking one missed payment is okay. Most creditors will report a missed payment as soon as the payment is one month late. This situation already has a negative effect on your credit score. The more payments you miss, the worse your credit score becomes. After six months of non-payment, the creditor will hand over your account to debt collectors. Once you get to this stage, your credit score will decrease rapidly. *After 30 days your credit score can start to decrease due to poor financial decisions.*

Myth: Paying collection accounts will increase your credit score quickly.

Truth: You should always pay your accounts on time or as soon as possible after missing a payment. Bad debts that you have not paid are eventually handed over to debt collection agencies and those debts are called collection accounts. Many people pay their collection accounts as debt collectors can become quite a nuisance with frequent phone calls and even making home visits. If you have a collection account, then your credit score will already have taken a knock since your payment history is poor. Paying a collection account will have an impact on your credit record – it will show the debt has been paid.

However, the non-payment will stay on your credit record for 7 years and only as it ages will the credit score improve. The latest FICO and VantageScore models provide an exception for debts less than $100; paying these collection accounts will result in it being removed from your credit record. *It may take up to 7 years for your credit score to increase after paying a collection account.*

Myth: Only some unpaid accounts will be shown on my credit record.

Truth: Lending institutions are responsible for reporting information to credit bureaus. They report both positive and negative transactions, but what the creditors report is entirely their own discretion. Some creditors might not report transactions, for example, small debts being owed may be written off and never reported. So there is no a 100% sure way to know which unpaid accounts are being reported to the credit bureaus. Home loan providers, financial institutions and rental companies usually report all transactions. Sometimes places like libraries will report late fines to the credit bureaus. *The reporting of unpaid accounts depends on the lending institution.*

Other Myths

Myth: A creditor will see the same score as you do.

Truth: The score you receive is from a credit scoring website based on a soft pull. A hard pull request by a lending institution may give the creditor a different score. The difference is due to the dynamic nature of scores and the different scoring models. Each institution will be using a preferred scoring model and there is no guarantee that it will be the same one you used. Creditors also obtain their information from credit bureaus and not credit scoring websites, so slight differences may exist. You can always ask the creditor which score they use if you want to get more information. *The credit score seen by a creditor is different from the one you see for many reasons.*

Myth: Savings accounts and debit cards improve your credit score.

Truth: Many people think that savings accounts, investment accounts, debit (checking) cards, and prepaid cards will increase a credit score. This assumption is incorrect since these types of accounts have no credit aspect and cannot form part of your credit score. Prepaid and debit card transactions are not reported to the credit bureaus and make it impossible to be added to your credit score. It only helps to increase your cash flow. A secured credit card is a better option if you want to build credit. *Financial products that impact your credit score are credit accounts and loans.*

Myth: Only one credit score exists for each person.

Truth: If you have read the previous chapters then you know that more than one score exists for each person since there are several credit scoring models. Your Fico and VantageScore ratings may be similar but they will not be identical, showing that more than one score exists. Other less popular models also exist for credit scores. A separate credit score is also available from each of the credit bureaus. *A credit score exists for every type of scoring model.*

Myth: Credit reports show identical information.
Truth: Equifax, Experian, and TransUnion all use their own information when calculating your credit score. Not all lending companies will report to all three credit bureaus; some will only report to one or two of the credit bureaus. The details on your credit report will differ from bureau to bureau. For that reason, you should request a report from each bureau annually to see how they compare and to check for any errors. *Details on credit reports differ between the credit bureaus.*

Summary

Many myths exist about credit scores and you should be aware of these myths. Most of the misconceptions regarding credit scores are a result of a person not being aware of how a credit record and scoring actually works. Only the credit model factors are considered as truth. It does not mean that the myths are total nonsense. In fact, many of the myths have just been misunderstood: they are more applicable to credit applications rather than credit scores.

We identified myths about demographics, applying for new credit streams, misconceptions regarding the credit score factors, and myths about bad credit. Now that the truth about each myth has been uncovered, you can move forward with your credit management and obtaining an exceptional credit score. If you are faced with a question regarding your credit score, always ask yourself if the new information would fall under one of the credit scoring factors. If the answer is negative then you can be certain it is a myth.

Credit Counseling and Financial Advising

Credit counselors and financial advisors are people who can help you to manage your finances. A financial adviser is more concerned with your future savings and investments. A credit counselor provides people with support on how to manage credit and their debts. Some people make use of both services to ensure their finances stay in top shape. Other people only turn to credit counselors when they are in trouble and are losing control of their debts. Either way, you may want to see a credit counselor at some point in time so here is some information to help you in making a suitable decision.

Credit counseling is sometimes referred to as debt counseling. These terms are quite similar since you have a debt that needs to be paid to a creditor. You have credit available but once you use it, it becomes known as a debt. The debt counseling process helps people to settle their debts through budgeting and financial training while making tools available to gradually reduce payments to creditors. You should never feel ashamed of going for debt counseling. Millions of people make use of these services every year. You are taking responsibility for your situation by seeking out help to take back control of your finances.

Signs you may need Credit Counselling

Most people will have some financial constraints during their lives. Extra expenses can pop up without any warning. You may have been in a car accident that leads to excessive hospital expenses, or is retrenched and no longer have an income. We all have times when money is tight or have no option but to live from paycheck to paycheck. But sometimes financial responsibilities just become too much and you may need to call in some help. There are some warnings you can look out for, which may indicate that you need to consult a credit counselor.

Sometimes money becomes tight and you know you won't be able to cover all your monthly expenses. You start to **use credit to pay for everyday expenses** like gas or food. When that happens, you won't have control over your budget and costs quickly compound into a large amount. You need to use all your money to pay off your credit card, which means that you **cannot save any money** for the future. If your savings are depleted and you have excessive debt then you need to start reviewing your financial strategy.

Another big sign is taking out additional loans to pay for current credit. This may happen in many ways but in essence, you are **using one form of a credit to pay for other debts**. There are many examples of this issue. You may be using money from your credit card to pay your store account, or you borrow money from a family member to pay your vehicle installment. You are just adding more debt to your current debt and still have a responsibility to pay the money back.

One of the key signs that you have financial problems is missing payments often. Once you get **behind on payments** it becomes quite difficult to catch up since you essentially need to save for additional installments. Playing catch-up becomes problematic and many people make the mistake of thinking it will just be one payment. You are going to need help to get your bills paid without making even more debt.

Services offered by Credit Counsellors

Most credit counselors offer several services. You need to determine which services are best for your needs and can help you to get out of debt. Generally speaking, credit counselors offer five main services:

- **Budget advice**: the counselor will discuss your income, expenses, and debt. The best financial strategy for you will then be explained by the counselor. In most cases, you will then need to go for follow-up sessions to have a personalized plan created for you. The credit counselor will also consider other services that can help you get out of a sticky situation.
- **Debt management**: the credit counselor will explain debt consolidation options to you. Debt consolidation is a process where your debts owed to various companies are combined (consolidated) into one debt. Usually, this debt will have a relatively low-interest rate and you get several years to pay off the debt based on a single monthly installment. The credit counseling company will negotiate this agreement and possibly lowering debts owed with your creditors.
- **Bankruptcy consultation**: a credit counselor can explain how the bankruptcy process works and help decide if this is the best option for you. The credit counselor will guide you

through all the steps and set you up with the correct people. You can also see the credit counselor after the bankruptcy process to help you plan for the future.
- **Student loan advice**: many people take out loans to pay for their studies but then struggle to pay back the debt. This situation is unfortunate since it can impact on obtaining other credit. A credit counselor can help to set up a repayment plan and negotiate with the lending institution on your behalf.
- **Accommodation counseling**: sometimes you may struggle to pay for your home, whether it is rent or a home loan. Credit counseling can help you to find the best payment options for you and keep your installments up to date.

Some of these services will have costs involved and some are free. The best option is to call several companies and find out what their fees are before proceeding with a booking. You shouldn't waste money on an unsuccessful counseling session, especially if your funds are already tight. A good idea is to call the credit counselor and ask what the costs are for the first consultation. If the first appointment is free then make a booking. Use the consultation to gauge if the credit counselor is someone you can work within the future before committing to paid services.

Advantages of Credit Counselling

Initially, you may think that going for credit counseling is a shame and means you have failed in your finances. You will quickly realize that it might be one of the best decisions you have ever made.

There are many benefits to going for credit counseling or visiting a financial advisor.
Firstly, you will learn how to **manage your finances** effectively. It teaches you prudent financial behavior and how to budget. You will learn more about the best ways to deal with credit and how to maintain a suitable credit-utilization ratio. A counselor will help you understand your credit record and to improve your credit score.
The credit counselor will **negotiate with creditors** on your behalf. This service can help you quite a lot since often you do not want to deal with creditors. You have probably already experienced a barrage of phone calls from creditors and received threatening letters. The last thing you want to do is to negotiate with a creditor. Luckily, the credit counselor will handle all communication with creditors. Credit counselors can help you with other negotiations as well. They can discuss the option of **paying lower interest rates** on any credit and store accounts.
Another benefit is the possibility to drastically **reduce late penalties** and extra charges on your accounts. The biggest benefit of debt counseling is the ability to finish paying off your debts faster. No one wants to struggle with debt forever and the **opportunity to become debt-free** is available with credit counseling. You will be taught how to manage your finances and improve your credit score. Another huge benefit is that you do not need to file for bankruptcy if you can get your debt under control.

Disadvantages of Credit Counselling

There are always disadvantages with anything you do and credit counseling is no different. Sometimes credit counseling **doesn't work but this is often times the indebted person's fault**. After receiving a debt management plan they try to venture off on their own and think they can handle their finances independently. Unfortunately, many people cannot do this and end up being unable to pay any debts, which ultimately ends in bankruptcy.

Lending institutions will also consider you to be a risk. Your **creditworthiness is in question** and poor decisions will remain on your credit record for many years to come. So you may not experience financial freedom as quickly as you might think.

Another disadvantage is that you will be **paying debts back for several years** to come. Additionally, someone else will be managing your finances so you do not have the liberty to spend money as you please. Most people spend between 3 and 5 years paying back their debt, during which time your own financial decisions are limited.

Finding a Reputable Credit Counsellor

There are several things to consider before deciding on a credit counselor. You may have heard some people saying you should stay away from debt counseling because it is a scam, or for some other reason. With any service, there are service providers who are not up to standard and may take chances. The best option is to do thorough research to ensure you get the best credit counselor possible.

Most credit counseling agencies are non-profit companies so watch out for companies that claim they make a profit. This situation shows they are gaining money and means you may be paying additional fees rather than saving money. The best way to check for the authenticity of a company is to ask for their **certification and accreditation**. The correct documentation indicates the agency is reputable and can be trusted with your case. The company should have a membership with the **Financial Counseling Association of America** or the **National Foundation for Credit Counseling**. Set standards must be adhered to by the credit counselor if they are a member of these societies. The Counsels also check up on the organizations and revise accreditation every few years.

Credit counseling can occur in several ways and you need to find the method that is best for you. Services are available via **phone, email, or in person**. Your available time and preferred communication method will help you determine the best option. For example, a person working an 8-hour job and spending time in traffic may find an email service to be best. In contrast, someone who recently became unemployed may decide to visit a credit counselor in person.

The cost of the service is another item to consider when choosing a credit counselor. The **prices of services vary** greatly so you need to consider costs in advance. The best option is to go for a free first consultation where the credit counselor will then provide a quote for further services. Keep in mind that the quotation may seem like an additional cost but weigh that up against not using the service and the potential of poor financial decisions. You may just save your credit score by seeing someone sooner rather than later.

In most cases, credit counseling is free so you should be extremely wary of people who charge fees for their

services, especially if they are not accredited at one of the institutions. In fact, stay away from anyone who is not accredited. Non-profit credit counselors provide free services and tend to provide services since they know they cannot gain any additional income. Additionally, the counselors are generally friendlier and provide better service. **Non-profit credit counselors** will attempt to find the most cost-effective solution to your financial situation. Remember that you're responsible for your situation and need to give all your effort when working with a credit counselor. One way to take control is to have all your information together. You need to be honest about your finances for a counselor to help you find the best plan for your future. Compile a list of all your debts to take with for your first meeting. Additionally, take along your latest payslip and any other income information you may have. A list of all your assets (house, vehicle, valuable art, etc.) should be included to help the credit counselor see if there is an easy solution to the situation. Keep in mind that the advice might not be what you want to hear but can get you out of a pickle quickly. For example, if your total debt is $10,000 and you have a classic car worth $12,000 then selling the vehicle can get rid of your debt.
The following list of questions should be asked of any credit counselor. The answers will give you a clear indication of whether the person can help you, or if you should move on to the next option.

- What services are available from your organization? The more services a company offers the better the chances of finding a suitable solution. Most people want to avoid a

debt management plan (DMP) so steer away from an organization that immediately proposes this as a first solution.
- Do you have educational information available? Most credit counselors will have a lot of information to help you understand the processes and how to get out of debt. Any company asking you to pay for information should not be used for credit counseling.
- Can you help me out of my current dilemma and provide assistance for the future? A good credit counselor will give you a strategy to get out of debt and a plan to help you manage your finances better in the future.
- How much do your services cost? You want to go for a free service but if you do decide on a paid credit counselor then check what fees are required from you. Some charge a set-up or administration fee, while other counselors require a monthly service fee. Ask for a written quote of the fees to ensure you do not pay more than necessary.
- What happens if I cannot pay the required fees? You want to save money and sometimes cannot afford to pay the credit counselor's fees. Ask this question to know what would happen if you cannot make a payment towards the counselor's account. If the company isn't willing to help then you should rather choose a different credit counselor.
- Are there any documents to sign? Some companies require you to sign paperwork for various reasons. Read all of the paperwork

and ask to have someone else review the documents with you. Never sign anything based on trust alone. If the credit counselor makes any promises then you should ask for the agreements in writing and ensure it is signed by the relevant people.
- What qualifications do your counselors have? Ask about their training and accreditation. Ask to see the accreditation documents of the company and respective counselors.
- How do you keep my personal information private? You do not want your data leaked or shared with third parties. The organization should have secure storage facilities and keep your data confidential at all times.

Credit counseling is a service available to people to take back control of their credit facilities, oftentimes due to high credit balances. There are a lot of different signs to indicate you may need credit counseling. You may need credit counseling if you are using credit for daily expenses, cannot save money, your payments are falling behind, or you are using credit to pay other debts. Credit counselors can provide you with advice and strategies on budgets, debt management, and accommodation costs. Additionally, they can help you with consolidating debts, help with payment strategies for student loans, and explain bankruptcy procedures.

The advantages of credit counseling include improved financial management, lower interest rates, and reduction of fees. The biggest benefit is the ability to become debt-free. The disadvantages of credit counseling are that you will spend several years to pay back debts, and some lenders will question your creditworthiness. Additionally, there are instances where credit counseling does not work.

The real key to success is finding a reputable credit counselor with certification and accreditation. You can use the questions provided in this book to help you find a reputable credit counselor. Credit counseling services are mostly free, but there may be some fees involved with extensive services. The credit counselor will help you get your finances under control, but it is still your responsibility to follow through with the given suggestions.

Final Thoughts

At the beginning of this book, you saw two scenarios: Peter who was using credit irresponsibly and faced major problems, and Joe and Mary who were using credit strategies to improve their credit scores and secured a home loan. Think about each scenario for a moment. What should Peter do to get out of his debt problems? Why are Joe and Mary a good example of responsible credit users?

After reading the previous chapters you can now understand why credit scores are extremely important and how it affects a person's daily life. Spend a few minutes thinking about your own spending habits and how you use your credit facilities. What is your current credit score? In which areas could you improve your credit score? You have probably already thought about these types of questions as you read the book, but now is the time to put your thoughts into action. Here is a quick wrap-up of the book and a few tips to get you started on your new credit building journey. Refer to the section titled "Learn the lingo" if you are uncertain about any word used frequently throughout the text.

A credit score is a number assigned to an individual (or business) that explains how well you work with the money that is lent to you. A high credit score is always better and indicates that you are a reliable person who pays back what is due to a lender. A credit record (or report) is a detailed account of your personal information, credit history, public filings, and current credit obligations. Your credit record is an important document and is used by financial institutions to help decide if they can trust you with their money.

Your credit score can be determined through various credit scoring models. Several models exist throughout the world, but the most common ones remain FICO and VantageScore. Each model has select factors used in calculating the credit score and assigns a weighting to every factor. FICO and VantageScore are used prolifically by lending institutions, as well as the three main credit bureaus. A personal credit score will be between 300 and 850. A person with a score in the high 700s will be an attractive customer for credit agencies. A high credit score can have many benefits. You can negotiate better deals, qualify for additional credit more easily, and be offered some of the best credit terms available. Additionally, you have bragging rights and should feel proud of your accomplishment!

Frequent credit score checks are very important. You should check your credit score and record at least once every year to verify that all the information is correct. This check will help with identifying instances of identity fraud and can help you prepare for credit applications that will be made in the future. Each person is entitled to receiving one free credit report per year from a credit bureau. You can request additional reports throughout the year but it will cost you a few bucks.

A person who wants to increase a credit score can do it in several ways. You can improve the credit score for each factor by following general guidelines. The most important thing to remember is to always pay your bills on time. This single thing can make or break your credit record. You should also avoid behaviors that can reduce your credit score. Do not take on more debt than you can payback.

Credit score myths are things you hear about what affects credit scores, or how credit scores are used in practice. There are many myths but most of them are not true at all and have no impact on your credit score. Always seek out the truth surrounding these myths. Some of the myths do ring true but are being applied incorrectly to the credit score calculation. In most cases, the myth is only relevant to a credit application. Carefully analyze any information you may receive that does not seem correct.

If your credit situation has gotten out of control, or you feel like you are drowning in debt, then it may be the time to see a credit counselor. They can help you to create an action plan and to sort out your debts. The plan may include debt consolidation, lowering fees, and creating a payment plan. But remember that you remain responsible for your debts, and only you can get yourself out of this situation.

We hope this book has given you clarity regarding credit scores and how to build credit. It is possible to have a high credit score and a solid credit record. Apply the teachings in this book and you will see an improvement in your credit score within a few months. Use these strategies on a daily basis and enjoy a fruitful credit future!

www.ingramcontent.com/pod-product-compliance
Lightning Source LLC
Chambersburg PA
CBHW020544220526
45463CB00006B/2185